DATE DUE

		ᘒᏮ	

KWEISI
MFUME

The African-American Biographies Series

MARIAN ANDERSON
Singer and Humanitarian
0-7660-1211-5

MAYA ANGELOU
More Than a Poet
0-89490-684-4

LOUIS ARMSTRONG
King of Jazz
0-89490-997-5

ARTHUR ASHE
Breaking the Color Barrier
in Tennis
0-89490-689-5

BENJAMIN BANNEKER
Astronomer and Mathematician
0-7660-1208-5

JULIAN BOND
Civil Rights Activist and Chairman of the NAACP
0-7660-1549-1

RALPH BUNCHE
Winner of the Nobel Peace Prize
0-7660-1203-4

BESSIE COLEMAN
First Black Woman Pilot
0-7660-1545-9

W. E. B. DU BOIS
Champion of Civil Rights
0-7660-1209-3

PAUL LAURENCE DUNBAR
Portrait of a Poet
0-7660-1350-2

DUKE ELLINGTON
Giant of Jazz
0-89490-691-7

ARETHA FRANKLIN
Motown Superstar
0-89490-686-0

NIKKI GIOVANNI
Poet of the People
0-7660-1238-7

WHOOPI GOLDBERG
Comedian and Movie Star
0-7660-1205-0

LORRAINE HANSBERRY
Playwright and Voice of Justice
0-89490-945-2

MATTHEW HENSON
Co-Discoverer of the North Pole
0-7660-1546-7

LANGSTON HUGHES
Poet of the Harlem Renaissance
0-89490-815-4

ZORA NEALE HURSTON
Southern Storyteller
0-89490-685-2

JESSE JACKSON
Civil Rights Activist
0-7660-1390-1

QUINCY JONES
Musician, Composer, Producer
0-89490-814-6

BARBARA JORDAN
Congresswoman, Lawyer,
Educator
0-89490-692-5

CORETTA SCOTT KING
Striving for Civil Rights
0-89490-811-1

MARTIN LUTHER KING, JR.
Leader for Civil Rights
0-89490-687-9

KWEISI MFUME
Congressman and NAACP Leader
0-7660-1237-9

TONI MORRISON
Nobel Prize-Winning Author
0-89490-688-7

WALTER DEAN MYERS
Writer for Real Teens
0-7660-1206-9

JESSE OWENS
Track and Field Legend
0-89490-812-X

COLIN POWELL
Soldier and Patriot
0-89490-810-3

A. PHILIP RANDOLPH
Union Leader and Civil Rights Crusader
0-7660-1544-0

PAUL ROBESON
Actor, Singer, Political Activist
0-89490-944-4

JACKIE ROBINSON
Baseball's Civil Rights Legend
0-89490-690-9

BETTY SHABAZZ
Sharing the Vision
of Malcolm X
0-7660-1210-7

HARRIET TUBMAN
Moses of the Underground Railroad
0-7660-1548-3

MADAM C. J. WALKER
Self-Made Businesswoman
0-7660-1204-2

IDA B. WELLS-BARNETT
Crusader Against Lynching
0-89490-947-9

OPRAH WINFREY
Talk Show Legend
0-7660-1207-7

CARTER G. WOODSON
Father of African-American History
0-89490-946-0

—African-American Biographies—

KWEISI MFUME

Congressman and NAACP Leader

Series Consultant:
Dr. Russell L. Adams, Chairman
Department of Afro-American Studies, Howard University

M. Elizabeth Paterra

Enslow Publishers, Inc.

40 Industrial Road   PO Box 38
Box 398   Aldershot
Berkeley Heights, NJ 07922   Hants GU12 6BP
USA   UK
http://www.enslow.com

921
mfu
c.1
2002
18.85

Library of Congress Cataloging-in-Publication Data

Paterra, M. Elizabeth.
    Kweisi Mfume : congressman and NAACP leader / M. Elizabeth Paterra.
        p. cm. – (African-American biographies)
    Includes bibliographical references and index.
    Summary: Follows the life of the current president of the National Association for the Advancement of Colored People from the gang-plagued streets of Baltimore, Maryland, to his position of leadership in Congress and among the African-American community.
    ISBN 0-7660-1237-9
    1. Mfume, Kweisi—Juvenile literature. 2. Legislators—United States—Biography—Juvenile literature. 3. Afro-American Legislators—Biography—Juvenile literature. 4. Afro-Americans—Biography—Juvenile literature. 5. United States. Congress. House—Biography—Juvenile literature. 6. Afro-Americans—Politics and government—Juvenile literature. 7. National Association for the Advancement of Colored People—Biography—Juvenile literature.
    [1. Mfume, Kweisi. 2. Legislators. 3. Afro-Americans—Biography.]
    I. Title. II. Series.
    E840.8.M5 P37   2000
    323'.092 – dc21

    00-008029

Printed in the United States of America

10 9 8 7 6 5 4 3 2 1

To Our Readers:
We have done our best to make sure all Internet addresses in this book were active and appropriate when we went to press. However, the author and the publisher have no control over and assume no liability for the material available on those Internet sites or on other Web sites they may link to. Any comments or suggestions can be sent by e-mail to comments@enslow.com or to the address on the back cover.

Illustration Credits: Courtesy of the Baltimore Sun, pp. 55, 58, 62, 68, 78; Courtesy of the National Association for the Advancement of Colored People (NAACP), pp. 6, 89; M. Elizabeth Paterra, pp. 12, 15, 17, 18, 30, 35, 39, 44, 48, 72; Photo courtesy of Mrs. Leavonia McKnight, pp. 21, 26.

Cover Illustration: Courtesy of the National Association for the Advancement of Colored People (NAACP).

CONTENTS

Kweisi Mfume

1

TAKING CHANCES, MAKING CHOICES

ighteen-year-old Frizzell Gray stood on a street corner in West Baltimore in the middle of the territory ruled by a neighborhood gang. It was muggy on that August evening in 1966, and he was about to do something he did not want to do. Still, he knew his own survival depended on the action he was about to take. To become one of the gang, he had to follow a drunk down a side street, mug him, and steal his wallet.

Frizzell spied his intended victim and started toward him. He had no desire to hurt the drunk, but when the man fought back, Frizzell hit him. After a struggle, Frizzell grabbed the man's wallet and darted back to the gang, flashing his prize. He accomplished his mission, and the gang accepted him. After that initiation, fighting and life on the streets became second nature to Frizzell.[1]

Thirty years later, on February 15, 1996, Frizzell Gray—with a new, West African name, Kweisi Mfume, which means "conquering son of kings"—stepped forward to accept another mission that would change his life. As a five-term congressman from Maryland, Mfume left his seat in the House of Representatives to be sworn in as the head of the National Association for the Advancement of Colored People (NAACP).

The NAACP, one of the oldest and most influential civil rights groups in the country, needed new leadership. It would not be an easy job for Mfume. The organization was struggling under shrinking membership and a debt of more than $3 million. Mfume would have to restructure the NAACP and clear it of its debt. He would also have to inspire other civil rights organizations to get involved.

On this crisp February day, Mfume moved to center stage at the National Press Club in Washington, D.C. President Bill Clinton and Vice President Al Gore shared the platform with him. Mfume spoke to a room filled with government dignitaries and members of the press. He said that he had been chosen to lead the NAACP back to the "front line in the continuing battle for racial equality."[2] Mfume urged young people to become involved—and to be accountable for their own actions. "The time is now," he said, "for a new generation to join the NAACP. While we value maturity and experience, we must also learn to cherish youth."[3]

Mfume's motto is "As long as the finish line is ahead, you always have the ability to shape your life, no matter who you are."[4] Becoming president and chief executive officer of the NAACP made Mfume one of the most important African-American leaders today. His goals were to center his energies on increasing the political power of the NAACP and the African-American community, and to help his people attain educational excellence and economic equality.[5] Mfume's road to this position was not an easy one, and the work that lay ahead would test his leadership skills, but he was eager and ready for the task.

2

GROWING UP IN TURNERS STATION

rizzell Gray, the first child of Mary Elizabeth Willis, was born on October 24, 1948. His father was Charles Tate, but Charles and Mary never married. Because he was such a small baby, Frizzell's aunt Alice began to call him Pee Wee. Several of his childhood friends still call him by that nickname today. Frizzell's mother later married Clifton Gray, and they had three daughters. Darlene was born in 1950; LaWana in 1951; and Michele in 1955. As a child, Frizzell thought that Clifton Gray was his father.

Frizzell lived his early years in Turners Station, Maryland. Turners Station was a quiet African-American community across the railroad tracks from the white town of Dundalk, near Baltimore. People from both towns worked at the nearby Bethlehem Steel plant and the Sparrows Point shipyards, but African Americans could live only in Turners Station. Segregation of the races was legal at that time. Signs in Dundalk said "whites only," and most stores and restaurants had separate drinking fountains and bathrooms for whites and blacks.[1]

Clifton Gray, Frizzell's stepfather, worked part-time as a truck driver. The family lived in a well-kept town-house complex called Day Village in the center of Turners Station. Each group of town homes formed an enclosed court where neighbors could chat and children could play kickball or practice pitching and hitting baseballs, often under the watchful eye of caring adults.[2]

Mary Gray did all she could to give her children a happy childhood. The children bustled about their mother whenever she made cookies. Mary let each child sample the dough and gave them empty jelly glasses to cut out cookie shapes. One of Frizzell's favorite treats was pineapple upside-down cake. He still requests this cake whenever there is a holiday or special family celebration.[3]

Mary Gray also taught her children important life lessons. "One of the most valuable lessons my mother taught me was to fight back," he later recalled. One

As a child, Mfume's name was Frizzell Gray. He was born in the small town of Turners Station, Maryland.

time, when he was eight or nine, Frizzell ran home to avoid a fight with the neighborhood bully, Big Neal. Frizzell's mother met him at the door and ordered him to go back and defend his honor. After the fight,when both boys dropped from exhaustion, Frizzell knew "fighting back was important, not just in society, but in terms of life."[4]

Frizzell enjoyed reading comic books and weightlifting magazines, but his mother made sure he was exposed to more serious literature, too. Reading and education were very important to Mary Gray. She would read to Frizzell and his sisters from *Devotions Upon Emergent Occasions, Meditation 17,* a famous poem by the seventeenth-century English poet John Donne. Donne's words taught Frizzell that no one is really alone. Part of the poem reads:

> *No man is an island,*
> *Entire of itself;*
>
> *Every man is a piece of the continent,*
> *A part of the main . . .*
>
> *Any man's death diminishes me,*
> *Because I am involved in mankind . . .*[5]

Mary Gray also talked about the importance of civil rights. She taught Frizzell about civil rights leaders and other African-American heroes who fought to end segregation, people such as A. Philip Randolph.[6] As the head of the first labor union for African-American workers, Randolph worked for equal opportunity, equal pay, and equal treatment. He spoke out against discrimination in the armed forces during World War II, and in 1963 he spearheaded the March on Washington for Jobs and Freedom.

The mid-1950s was a very important time for the civil rights movement. Lawyers for the National Association for the Advancement of Colored People (NAACP) fought in court to outlaw discrimination based on the color of a person's skin. In 1954, the Supreme Court ruled in the *Brown* v. *Board of Education of Topeka, Kansas* case that it was illegal to have separate schools for black and white children. In 1955, Rosa Parks of Montgomery, Alabama, became a hero for many when she refused to give her seat to a white passenger and move to the back of the bus. Inspired by this victory, more and more African Americans began to speak out. Mary Gray quizzed her children so they would always remember the important people involved in gaining civil rights for African Americans.

Across the concrete drive from Frizzell's house lived Carl Swann, Frizzell's best friend. Frizzell, Carl, and their friend Vernon Turner often went fishing, organized ball games, and collected empty soda bottles to turn in for two cents each at the candy store. Frizzell loved collecting empty soda bottles and vied with his buddies for the title King of the Bottle Hustlers—the lucky one who collected the most bottles. Really, though, everyone was a winner because after the competition the kids pooled their money and enjoyed bags of coconut cookies, chewy Squirrel Nut candy, and soda. When a carnival came to town, the bottle money bought tickets for rides and treats. People in the community still talk about the three friends gathered in the summertime under the shade of three pine trees behind Frizzell's house to play cards and to talk about baseball and fishing.[7]

But sometimes events at Frizzell's home did not go smoothly. One of the problems Frizzell faced was the

Frizzell lived here in Day Village. His friends Carl Swann and Vernon Turner lived across the courtyard.

anger of his stepfather, Clifton Gray. Not only did Gray yell at and even hit his wife, he was especially mean to Frizzell. Ronald Turner, Vernon's brother, once described an incident when Frizzell's mother was working and Clifton Gray was home with the children. "Clifton charged out of the house, grabbed Frizzell by the neck and dragged him home to scrub the floor," Turner said.[8] Other times, when Mary Gray was not around, Clifton Gray would yell at Frizzell and hit him. Frizzell prayed that his stepfather would leave them alone. It would be many years before that prayer was answered.

Apart from dealing with his abusive stepfather, Frizzell's childhood was a happy one. He attended Fleming Elementary School, and he was a good student. He also did his share of teasing the girls, pulling their braids and then denying he had done it. "He was always articulate and could talk his way out of anything," a classmate said later.[9]

In 1957, when Frizzell was nine, his mother signed him up for the Turners Station Little League baseball team organized by Osceola Smith. Smitty, as he was called, charged each player $7.50 per season to be on his team. This was a lot of money for Frizzell's family, but it included uniforms and equipment for the team. Smitty felt it was very important that the children of Turners Station not feel deprived when they played against white teams from wealthier communities.[10]

Smitty was a role model and a mentor for the boys, and Frizzell would always be grateful for the self-discipline and pride Smitty taught him. Smitty told him to practice twice as long and twice as hard as the others because he was not as strong as the bigger boys on the team. Frizzell followed that advice, and his success playing baseball became a source of pride.[11]

By the time Frizzell was eleven years old, his stepfather was drinking regularly. One day, Frizzell was so angry and upset with his stepfather's behavior that

On this field, Frizzell played third base for the Turners Station Yankees. "I never wanted to let my teammates down," he said.

he interrupted a fight between his parents. Clifton Gray threw Frizzell outside and locked the door, but Frizzell thrust his fist through the glass door, cutting himself. He was determined to stop Gray and protect his mother. He opened the door, grabbed a knife, and threatened his stepfather, telling him to leave and never come back. Sometime after that, Clifton Gray did leave. Then, in 1960, Mary Gray moved the family to West Baltimore, where she had grown up.

In 1960, the year Frizzell turned twelve, his family moved to a row house like these in West Baltimore.

3

WEST BALTIMORE

In West Baltimore, Frizzell and his family lived near his aunts and many other relatives. Life in West Baltimore was quite different from life in Turners Station. Instead of baseball, fishing, and collecting empty soda bottles, Frizzell spent his time looking after his sisters, selling the *Baltimore Afro-American* newspaper, and working at Dave's Grocery. Instead of a small town with few attractions, West Baltimore had the "strip," a street of stores, restaurants, nightclubs, and theaters. Black people there were "as classy as any whites I'd ever seen in Dundalk," Frizzell later remembered.[1]

West Baltimore could seem like a big and scary place for a twelve-year-old boy, but it also offered many new experiences. Frizzell loved walking around the city with Rufus "Rip" Tate, a friend of the family. During these walks, Mr. Charles, as the family called him, introduced Frizzell to West Baltimore. They would go into pool halls, and walk down the strip where everybody knew Rip. The two would walk for hours, sometimes talking, sometimes not. Still, Frizzell was never bored. If someone asked Tate whether Frizzell was his son, he would answer, "Yeah, he's my boy." At the time Frizzell did not suspect that Tate really was his father, but it still felt good to hear him say he was.[2]

This was also a difficult time for Frizzell's family. Mary Gray struggled to support the children by herself. She worked as an elevator operator and as a maid, but she did not earn much money. Sometimes Mr. Charles would help out, bringing money or bags of groceries. Other times, Mr. Pottash, the owner of Dave's Grocery, would let the Grays buy groceries on credit. At the store, Frizzell swept the floor and arranged food on the shelves. In time, he became friendly with Mr. Pottash and his family. Mr. Pottash, who was Jewish, told Frizzell of his experiences surviving the Holocaust, when Nazi dictator Adolf Hitler of Germany ordered the deaths of millions of Jews and others in Europe.[3]

Frizzell and his family were forced to move four

times in the next five years, whenever they were evicted for not paying their rent on time. Mary Gray struggled to provide structure and discipline for her children. To keep Frizzell out of trouble, Mary Gray enrolled him in the Falcon Drum and Bugle Corps. The band's purpose was to build good character and enhance musical talent in West Baltimore's boys. Under the leadership of strict, often impatient Arnette Evans, Frizzell learned to play the French horn. Evans used rough language with the boys and challenged them to do their best. Evans would lead long, tiring

Teenagers in the Falcon Drum and Bugle Corps performed at parades and other celebrations.

practices and scream anytime someone made a mistake. Some of the boys hated Evans, but most stayed in the corps to prove to him that they could do it.

When the Falcon Drum and Bugle Corps grew to seventy youngsters, Evans appealed to the Baltimore Public School System for a place to practice. The assistant superintendent was so impressed with the corps that he gave the group space at nearby Public School 112. They performed at parades and celebrations throughout Maryland, Pennsylvania, and West Virginia, and they even won first place in a competition with white groups in McSherrytown, Pennsylvania.[4]

Everyone in the neighborhood worked together to raise money for band instruments and uniforms. Neighbors collected three-day-old newspapers, scrap glass, and iron. They sold "conversational stones," small stones that they had handpainted and inscribed with Bible verses. They also sponsored candy and greeting card sales. "The boys ate as much candy as they sold," recalled one organizer of the corps.[5]

The Falcon Drum and Bugle Corps was not enough to keep Frizzell off the streets. Together with his new friend Gary Fenwick, Frizzell would wander around West Baltimore. "I'm just going over to Gary's," he would say to his mother.[6]

One warm fall evening in 1962, Frizzell decided to sneak out alone to hear President John F. Kennedy speak at the nearby armory. Frizzell had often heard his mother talk about President Kennedy, saying that he would help poor African Americans get better jobs, decent housing, and education.

That evening, Frizzell slipped out of his bedroom without his mother's knowledge and ran the five blocks to the armory. The crowds, the police cars, and the lights excited him. Never had he seen so many people gathered in one place. The event was bigger than any carnival or baseball game he had ever attended. Then he noticed that he appeared to be the only black person there. He hid behind the bleachers on the second floor where he could see everything, but the crowd could not see him.

Frizzell was impressed by the men in the crowd chomping on cigars and by the neatly dressed women holding their elegant hats in their hands. Red, white, and blue banners and streamers fluttered in the hot air. Frizzell could not believe his eyes.[7]

He sat as quietly as he could and listened to everything. Kennedy spoke about equal opportunities for all people, regardless of color. Even though he could not remember any of Kennedy's exact words later, Frizzell felt excited by the speeches and the crowd. The next morning, Frizzell told his mother of his adventure. She did not punish him for sneaking out of the house without her knowledge—instead, she scolded him for not inviting her to go along.[8]

Less than a year later, Frizzell learned how easy it was to get into trouble on the streets of West Baltimore. One hot summer evening in 1963, Frizzell and his best friend, Gary Fenwick, were hanging around near Mr. Pottash's store. Mr. Pottash's car, a highly prized shiny Plymouth was parked by the curb. Someone dared Gary to toss a lighted match through the window.

Frizzell was not sure what to do. He was a friend of the Pottashes. "They were part of the community and in many respects part of the extended family," he later said. Mr. Pottash had helped out his mother, and Frizzell had been invited into the Pottash's home. Frizzell did not want to see the Pottashes hurt, but he did not want to seem afraid in front of the other boys, either. He tried to talk Gary out of it. Then, suddenly, it was too late. Gary had thrown the match and the car had begun to burn.[9]

The police arrested both Frizzell and Gary. Since the boys were only fifteen, they were tried in juvenile court. Horrified, Frizzell's mother brought witnesses to tell the judge that Frizzell was really a good boy. She also forced Frizzell to apologize to the Pottash family. The judge let him off with only a warning, but Frizzell barely listened. He began to spend more and more time on the street, he let his school work slip, and he began drinking and smoking marijuana.

Still, many of the adults in his life did not give up on Frizzell. He continued to march with the Falcon Drum and Bugle Corps. His mother tried to spend her free time with Frizzell and his sisters, but she worked so much that they rarely saw her. Frizzell's teachers at his new junior high school also tried to keep him focused on school work. One day, walking down the hall at Booker T. Washington Junior High School, Frizzell told his friends how much he hated industrial arts class. He said learning how to use tools and machines was a waste of his time. As Frizzell roamed the halls, a man's burly shoulder bumped against him, backing him against the locker. "Which would you rather do, come to class or have it out with me?" boomed Mr. Rawlings, his industrial arts teacher. Frizzell had no difficulty understanding Mr. Rawlings's message and followed him to class. It was "fear added to this sense of order and discipline," he remembered, that helped him through eighth and ninth grade.[10]

At home with his mother, Frizzell continued to follow the progress of the civil rights movement. On August 28, 1963, at the March on Washington for Jobs and Freedom, Martin Luther King, Jr., delivered his memorable "I Have a Dream" speech. King was a well-known civil rights leader, and everyone was excited about the March on Washington. With their ears glued to the radio, Frizzell and his family listened to King's impassioned words. Mary Gray's eyes filled with tears

Frizzell, middle row left, wearing hat, poses with other members of the Falcon Drum and Bugle Corps after they won first prize in a contest in McSherrytown, Pennsylvania.

as she heard King say, "I have a dream that my four little children will live in a nation where they will not be judged by the color of their skin, but by the content of their character." Mary Gray had the same dream for her four children.[11]

Less than a year later, Frizzell faced the greatest crisis of his childhood. He learned that his mother had cancer and was dying. Mary Gray made her son promise to take care of his sisters. She told him, "No matter how hard things get, promise Mama you'll never give up, that you'll never settle for second best."[12] Frizzell promised. He hoped with all his heart that she would get better, but his wishes did not come true. She died in Frizzell's arms one night in April 1965. Frizzell was just sixteen.

Preparing for his mother's funeral was a dreadful experience for young Frizzell. During the funeral services, Frizzell had another shock. Rip Tate, the family friend known as Mr. Charles, told Frizzell that he was his real father. Frizzell and Tate talked for hours, but after that night Frizzell would see very little of his father. Tate did what he could for his family, but he was devastated by Mary Gray's death, and it would take him eight years of drug abuse and a trip to prison before he would get his life back together.[13]

Frizzell was faced with more troubles than he had ever known. His mother was gone. He had no money to support his sisters, who were fourteen, thirteen, and nine years old at the time. He feared that they would be sent to foster homes.[14] Frizzell dropped out of school and resigned from the Falcon Drum and Bugle Corps to find work. His worry about taking care of his sisters lessened a little when they moved in with their grandmother. Frizzell went to live with two divorced uncles.

4

LIFE ON
THE STREETS

rizzell's life was suddenly very lonely. The sixteen-year-old boy lived with his uncles but rarely saw them. Suddenly he had no adults in his life to give him advice or support.

Frizzell found an all-night job in a bakery, pushing bread through a machine that sliced and wrapped it. During the day he sold poultry and packed rabbit and chicken parts in ice at a nearby outdoor market. On Sundays he shined shoes for churchgoers. After being beaten and robbed one night, Frizzell bought a gun to protect himself. When he was not working, Frizzell spent most of his time hanging out on the streets with

Sixteen-year-old Frizzell worked at an outdoor market like this one. His job was to display chicken and rabbit parts for sale.

Gary and other friends. He had learned to play craps, a gambling game with dice, and he quickly became an expert.

Frizzell also tried to be his sisters' protector and sometimes gave them money for food and clothing. Once, when he heard that his stepfather, Clifton Gray, had hit his sister Michele, Frizzell became very angry. He and Gary went to Gray's apartment and started smashing his car with lead pipes. Frizzell chased Gray inside the house and shot at him with his gun. Frizzell was arrested and spent a night in jail. He was fined for attacking his stepfather. Still, he never regretted it, because after that Gray left the girls alone.[1] A few years later, Gray died.

By 1966, when Frizzell was eighteen, he had become a numbers runner. Numbers is a private gambling operation like a lottery, but it is illegal. Frizzell acted cool and businesslike as he took customers' bets. He wrote the numbers on small slips of paper so he could swallow them if the police caught him. It was a dangerous job, but Frizzell liked it because he could make much more money than he could working at the bakery.[2]

The 1960s was a decade of turmoil in the United States. President Kennedy was assassinated in 1963. The country was deeply involved in a war in Vietnam, but many Americans did not support this war. Like all young men his age, Frizzell had to register for the draft for military service. A lottery system was used to randomly select those called to fight, but luckily Frizzell's number was never called.

During this time, depressing news of the war in Vietnam and of street demonstrations and riots at home dominated Frizzell's world. This discouraged a strong sense of right or wrong. Frizzell did not want to kill anyone, but like the other tough guys on the street, he was prepared to use anything and everything to prove that he could if he wanted to.[3] Even at the parties where gang members gathered with girlfriends, fighting often broke out as rival gangs challenged one another and fought over the girls. At one such party, in June 1966, Frizzell met a young woman named Pauline and fell in love.

After early victories, the civil rights movement faced increasing difficulties. In the South, a growing number of civil rights activists were being intimidated, beaten, and even murdered. Some younger African-American leaders, such as Malcolm X and Stokely Carmichael, spoke angrily against racism and said that it was time for blacks to fight back when attacked. Using slogans like Black Power, Carmichael and Malcolm X found receptive audiences in many poor urban neighborhoods.

These tensions finally exploded on April 4, 1968. In Tennessee, the Reverend Martin Luther King, Jr., was shot by a white man. Frizzell remembered how important Dr. King's message of hope had been to his mother.[4] That message had been violently silenced. Following the assassination, riots broke out in Baltimore and throughout the country. Stores were looted and African-American neighborhoods were destroyed. Police began arresting anyone suspected of rioting, especially young African Americans like Frizzell.

On the second night of riots in Baltimore, as Frizzell stepped out on the street to look at the damage, he was arrested. He was brought to the armory where he had once heard President John F. Kennedy speak. When no one was looking, Frizzell climbed out a window and ran home through the burned-out neighborhood. After those events, he later wrote, "It was clear that West Baltimore would never be the same."[5]

A month after the riot, Pauline gave birth to Frizzell's first son, Donald. Only nineteen years old when he became a father, Frizzell cared about Donald and Pauline, but he had little money and no plans for the future. His life was on the streets, and partying with girls was part of it.

Later during that summer of 1968, a chance encounter set Frizzell on a pathway toward change. As Frizzell stood alone on a street corner, an older man approached him. Parren Mitchell was running for Congress. He was walking the streets to introduce himself to the people of West Baltimore and to gather support.

Tough-guy Frizzell greeted the politican with hostility. Flashing his gun at Mitchell, Frizzell said that no one could change what was happening on the streets. Mitchell replied that Frizzell should be part of the solution and not part of the problem. Then he handed Frizzell a business card and invited him to help in his campaign. Frizzell slipped the card into his pocket, even though he did not plan to contact Mitchell.

A few weeks later, Frizzell made a big decision. He

appeared at Parren Mitchell's campaign headquarters and volunteered to help. Handing out MITCHELL FOR CONGRESS pamphlets was Frizzell's first experience in the world of politics.[6] Although Parren Mitchell lost that election, in a later political run he would win a seat in Congress.

But Frizzell was not ready to give up his wild lifestyle and the lure of the streets of West Baltimore. Over the next two and a half years, Frizzell fathered four more children, three with other young women and a second child with Pauline. "I was out of control and didn't know it," he later admitted.[7]

Still, he knew that he had a responsibility to his children, and he loved them. Frizzell continued to work at low-paying jobs to support himself and his three sisters. He gave whatever money he could for the support of his five sons, Donald, Kevin, Keith, Michael, and Ronald. Whenever he was free, he visited them and their mothers on weekends. He later said that at this point in his life, he had "no hope for the future and no real idea of where I was going—I was poor, black, and in real trouble."[8]

One hot night, as Frizzell was playing cards and drinking with his buddies on a street corner, a strange and compelling vision took hold of him: He saw his mother's face.

> People thought I was crazy, but that night I left that corner and prayed and asked for God's forgiveness—I

Frizzell began hanging out on the streets of West Baltimore. "I was out of control and didn't know it," he said later.

made a very real promise to myself, to my mother, and to God that night—that if I could just get one more chance, I would do everything I could to make a difference.[9]

After that night, Frizzell walked away from the gambling and the violence of the streets of West Baltimore. Every day for months, the members of his gang and the people who once were his friends would beat him up, trying to force him back to his former life.

But Frizzell Gray had finally realized that he needed a total break.

Soon Frizzell took more steps toward changing his life. He enrolled in a night school class and began a program of studies in history, math, algebra, English, and science. Even though studying had always come easily to Frizzell, he had been away from school for a long time and working took time away from his studies. But in spite of these difficulties, he passed the General Educational Development test (GED) and earned his high school equivalency diploma within a year.

Frizzell entered the Community College of Baltimore in January 1972. He was proud of the fact that he never borrowed money for school or even applied for a scholarship. He had quit numbers running and paid his tuition by rebuilding starters and transmissions for cars and selling life insurance door-to-door.[10]

Frizzell was dating Linda Shields, a friend he had known for some time. Linda and Frizzell spent more and more time together, and on July 1, 1972, they were married at Brown's Memorial Baptist Church.

5

STEPPING FORWARD

rizzell Gray threw himself into campus life at the Community College of Baltimore (CCB), a two-year college. He concentrated on his studies and became a good student. Leaving his hardships behind became his objective, and he saw education as a way to get ahead. Gray later credited the Community College of Baltimore with leading him to a political career.[1]

Gray's life was very busy. He already had five children, and now he had a wife, his studies, and many campus activities. He helped organize the college's Black Student Union (BSU), and with the BSU he protested against Gulf Oil, which was investing money in South Africa. At the time, South Africa had a racist government, and the BSU did not want American companies to be involved in the South African economy.

To strengthen the effectiveness of the BSU, Gray became editor of the college newspaper. He used the newspaper and his vice presidency of the Black Student Union to push for a stronger black studies curriculum and, he said, to "shake things up at the college."[2]

In December 1972, Gray and the BSU wanted to invite the controversial civil rights leader Stokely Carmichael to speak to the students at the Community College of Baltimore. Carmichael's Black Power slogan frightened many whites. When the CCB administration refused to let Carmichael come as a guest speaker, Gray led a sit-down strike. He and his group took over the administration building and organized picket lines in front of the school. The college officials did not yield to the students' protests, but Frizzell Gray's reputation as an activist spread.

Gray did not limit his activism to the CCB campus. He went out into the community, giving speeches and handing out pamphlets throughout Baltimore. He was concerned about all the problems in the ghettos— drugs, illiteracy, hopelessness.

Next, Gray turned to radio to reach a broader

At the Community College of Baltimore, Frizzell started to "shake things up." His college experiences as an activist led him to choose a career in politics.

African-American audience. Back in 1967, he had run errands as a volunteer at WWIN. But his first real break in radio came in 1973 when he was allowed to read news reports for WEBB. Owned by recording star James Brown, WEBB was the only black-owned station in Baltimore. Infatuated with radio and wanting to make it his career, Gray tried to improve his way of speaking. He polished his style by spending many hours practicing in front of the mirror and talking into a tape recorder. At WEBB, Gray began hosting *Ebony Reflections*, a regular Sunday afternoon radio program. Besides Top 40 selections, Gray played music with messages for social change. He also played tapes of speeches by well-known African-American activists, such as the Reverend Martin Luther King, Jr., Malcolm X, and Stokely Carmichael, and poetry by Nikki Giovanni. Then he invited listeners to call in and talk about the problems facing African Americans in Baltimore.[3]

In 1973, Gray decided he needed a new name to reflect his new identity. Frizzell Gray became Kweisi Mfume (pronounced Kwah-EE-see Oom-FOO-may) as a way, he said, "to embrace his African heritage."[4] After returning from a trip to Ghana, his great-aunt Lizzy had suggested the name, which means "conquering son of kings."

Mfume finished his studies at CCB, graduating in 1973 with a two-year associate in arts degree. He then transferred his two years of college credits to complete his studies at Morgan State University (MSU) in Baltimore. Unlike the student population at CCB, most of the students at Morgan State were African Americans.

Unfortunately, Mfume's marriage was not working out. He and Linda had drifted apart, and they agreed to separate.[5] The marriage had been a mistake, but they remained friends.

At MSU, Mfume joined the Student Government Association and continued to be active on campus. During his two years there, Mfume helped bring such well-known speakers as Jesse Jackson, writer James

Baldwin, and political activist Angela Davis to the university. Mfume was also active in the effort to create the university's own radio station, WEAA. At this station, he continued to host a show, but he focused more and more on talk, not music. He took calls from his listeners and discussed issues in the news. Many of these discussions were about Baltimore politics, Mayor William Schaefer, and the decisions of the city council. Mfume's radio show gave people a public forum to air their opinions about unemployment, poor housing, the shortage of police, and uncollected garbage. After graduating from Morgan State University with a political science degree in 1976, Mfume became the WEAA program director.

WEAA listeners agreed with Mfume's complaints: West Baltimore residents paid taxes, but their potholes were not repaired, trash collection was irregular, and police protection was scarce. Public officials did not use enough tax money to serve the needs of people in the poorer sections of town. Instead, most of the money was spent on large projects in other parts of Baltimore. Mayor Schaefer wanted to bring big business to Baltimore. He developed projects like the construction of Harbor Place, a showplace of restaurants, hotels, and entertainment venues. But poor people, many of them in Mfume's listening audience, did not benefit from beautification programs like Harbor Place. Mfume decided it was time to turn talk into action: He would run for city council.

6

ENTERING THE PUBLIC ARENA

n December 1978, Mfume shocked the city council and the people of Baltimore. While visiting a council meeting, Mfume saw that Councilman Emerson Julian's seat was empty. Striding past the security guards, Mfume planted himself in the seat. "This seat will be mine!" he announced.[1] Television cameras captured the scene, and the story hit the newspapers and radio. Mfume began his campaign for city council with a bang of publicity. Many of his radio listeners supported his candidacy. They were ready for change in the city's government.

Mfume relished the idea of running for city council

and threw himself full force into campaigning. He thought he had a good chance against Emerson Julian. Then, suddenly, two months later, Julian died of a heart attack. Now, instead of running against one candidate, Mfume faced nine new candidates, all seeking Julian's seat. One strong opponent was Mary B. Adams. She emphasized creating job opportunities, dredging the harbor to accommodate large vessels, and subsidizing housing and education. Another candidate was Congressman Parren Mitchell's nephew, Michael Mitchell, who had been active in Baltimore politics since 1975.

Mfume knew that to win the election he would need a lot of help. Carl Swann, his longtime friend, headed a staff of campaign volunteers. Mfume and his staff took different routes through Baltimore and covered all the streets of the Fourth District. They talked with workers heading for their jobs, housewives sweeping their front steps, and unemployed people hanging around on street corners. Mfume and his volunteers promised a future with better jobs, housing, and education for the poor.

Mfume was energized by the idea of being a part of city government. As a councilman, he promised to speak up for legislation to help the people in his district. Mfume's campaign slogan was "Beat the Bosses."[2] Although he had plenty of self-confidence, Mfume did not have the funds to run a big campaign.

After he decided to run for city council, Mfume and his staff went door-to-door, talking to people in Baltimore's Fourth District.

For help, he turned to Raymond V. Haysbert, president of Parks Sausage Company. Parks Sausage was one of the few African-American–owned businesses in the city. Mfume told Haysbert that if he won the council seat, he wanted to clean up the neighborhoods of West Baltimore and stop rents from going up. He spoke of helping the poor people who could not afford higher rents, who were being evicted and becoming homeless. Although Haysbert agreed with Mfume about the need to help the poor and the black communities, he

believed that rent control might discourage new prop-
erty owners from investing in Baltimore. And new
investors, Haysbert said, meant more money in taxes
for Baltimore.[3]

By the end of their meeting, Haysbert agreed to
help Mfume, but not in the way Mfume anticipated.
Haysbert gave him advice, not money. He told Mfume
that if he wanted to be a politician, he had to look like
one: Shave his beard, cut his hair, and dress neatly in
white shirts and dark suits. He also told him to list ten
issues his people were concerned about and to learn
exactly what the city council was doing about them.
Haysbert said more people would vote for him if he
presented a better image. Mfume respected Haysbert
and followed his advice.

The next mentor Mfume found was Senator Verda
Welcome, the first black woman in the United States to
serve as a state senator. Mfume knew Senator Welcome
only by reputation. After a long interview, Welcome
told Mfume, "I think you might just be committed
enough to make a real and lasting difference."[4]
Senator Welcome's support gave Mfume the boost he
needed. Soon after, the *Baltimore Sun*, the *News-
American*, and the *Baltimore Afro-American* newspapers
endorsed Mfume.

On September 11, 1979, all the candidates were at
the polls, handing out brochures, shaking hands, and
trying to win last-minute votes. Throughout the city,

voters made their choices. As the polls closed, the results from each voting area were reported on the television news. Mfume's staff kept a tally of the numbers, and by 11:45 p.m., their tally showed that Mfume was one hundred votes ahead of Mary Adams, his nearest competitor.

Just as Mfume and his staff began to congratulate one another, the television flashed the news that Mary Adams was the winner by forty-six votes. "The numbers are wrong!" Mfume told his staff.[5]

On September 14, the *Baltimore Sun* announced that Adams had received twenty-five absentee votes and Mfume received twenty-four. This put Adams ahead by forty-seven votes. But Mfume and his staff still believed that Mfume had won the election, and they insisted on a recount of all the ballots. That night Carl Swann guarded the warehouse where the voting machines were stored to ensure that no one tampered with the results.[6] The next morning, the *Baltimore Sun* carried the following headline: "Fourth Recount puts Mfume over Adams." Mfume had won the election by only three votes. It was the closest election in Maryland history.

Mfume's radio audiences cheered along with his family and friends. Now it was up to Mfume to keep the promises of his campaign: to secure funds for public education, advance economic development in West

Baltimore, and institute other reforms to help the city's poor.

Mfume was sworn in the first week of December 1979. He began his work by fighting with Mayor Schaefer and the city council. He attacked Schaefer for not appointing African Americans to the city's boards and commissions. He complained that the mayor and the predominately white city council had too much power. He charged that nothing happened at the city council without the mayor's approval. Schaefer did not like Mfume's accusations, and the two men quickly grew to dislike each other. According to Mfume, "Things were done his way, or not done at all."[7]

On his radio show, Mfume said that there were two cities in Baltimore, one black and one white. In a short time, Mfume's show became an example of what Carl Swann called "people power."[8] Mfume told his listeners that as long as so few African Americans served on the city council, their problems would be ignored. Mayor Schaefer fought back by refusing to let Mfume take part in city council discussions. One day, the mayor threw Mfume out of the council meeting, telling him not to come back until he was prepared to discuss the issues without such heated emotions.

The relationship between Mfume and Schaefer only worsened with their endless arguing. In time, Mfume became so frustrated that he seemed to lash out at council members just because they were white.

He needed to learn how to deal effectively with the mayor and the council.

In 1982, Mfume enrolled in a master's program in political science at Johns Hopkins University. When he received his degree two years later, he had a firmer understanding of the political process. After fighting the mayor and other city council members for more than two years without success, Mfume finally realized that he would have to make compromises to get what he wanted.

Flags fly at City Hall, where council meetings in 1979 often echoed with the endless arguments of Councilman Mfume and Mayor Schaefer.

When the council needed to redraw the voting districts in Baltimore, Mfume worked with a white councilman from neighboring South Baltimore. They began by asking each other what their people needed most. Then they developed a compromise that extended the Fourth District, increasing the number of voters in Mfume's district while keeping the ethnic neighborhoods of South Baltimore together. The plan was accepted by the council and the mayor and was Mfume's first success as a politician.

In 1986, Mfume coauthored legislation to stop Baltimore from investing in companies that did business in South Africa. Millions of dollars from taxpayers and city employees had gone to these businesses, indirectly helping to support South Africa's racist government. Mfume asked other councilmen to vote for his bill and promised in return to vote for bills that were important to them.[9] Almost two decades after his first meeting with Parren Mitchell, Mfume had become an effective politician. In his years on the city council, he worked to improve community safety and to increase opportunities for minorities to develop businesses.

Now he was ready to move ahead again. Parren Mitchell was retiring as United States Representative of Maryland's Seventh District and Mfume planned to run for Mitchell's seat. If he won, Mfume would be dealing in Congress with legislation that would affect not just the city of Baltimore but all Americans.

7

MFUME TAKES ON CONGRESS

s he had before, candidate Kweisi Mfume went door-to-door, introducing himself and talking to the people of Baltimore about the problems of poverty, poor education, and unreasonable rents. He told the voters about his record of achievement as councilman and promised to be their voice in Washington.

Political campaigns rarely run smoothly, and this was no exception. The Reverend St. George Cross III, Mfume's rival for the seat in Congress, looked into Mfume's family background and uncovered information that he hoped would turn the public against Mfume.

In October 1986, candidates Mfume and Cross clashed in front of Lawrence G. Paquin School, a high school in Baltimore for pregnant inner-city girls. Pointing toward the young girls gathered behind him, Cross said they were not students at this school because they wanted to be. They attended Paquin because they were pregnant and unmarried. Then he pointed to Mfume and accused, "Now we have somebody who could have had several girls forced to attend classes in this building and he wants to be your congressman."[1] Cross wanted voters to view Mfume as irresponsible and a poor candidate because he had fathered five children out of wedlock.

Cross's accusation angered Mfume. Cross was using the mistakes of Mfume's youth as a weapon against him. Mfume had never kept this information from the public. He had tried to be a good father, taking his children to church, to ball games, and celebrating special occasions with them. Despite Cross's negative campaigning, when the polls closed on November 4, 1986, Mfume had won the election by a large majority.

In January 1987, Mfume, representing the Seventh Congressional District of Maryland, arrived on Capitol Hill in Washington, D.C., along with fifty other newcomers to Congress. Mfume found that as a new congressman, he was a small fish in a large pond. He understood that doing an effective job in Congress depended on establishing positive relationships with his fellow members. He began by memorizing the names and backgrounds of key members of both the House of Representatives and the Senate.

Mfume volunteered to be speaker pro tem. The speaker pro tem substitutes for the Speaker of the House when the elected Speaker is not available. Many senior representatives did not want this time-consuming job, but as a new congressman, Mfume saw it as an opportunity to learn the many details of congressional procedure. He also knew that presiding over congressional debates would help him become better known by the other congressmen.

Two thousand or more laws, or changes to laws, are proposed to Congress each year, and Congress has a variety of committees to consider all these proposals. Each committee has a special area of expertise.

Like all members of Congress, Mfume was assigned to two committees and some subcommittees. His first year, he was appointed to the Banking, Finance, and Urban Affairs Committee and to the Small Business Committee. He knew little about these areas, so he spent much of his first term reading and learning about banking and business issues. He wanted to be well informed so he could contribute to the discussions over the laws that would be debated by these committees.

Mfume also joined the Congressional Black Caucus (CBC), a group of African-American congressmen who banded together to vote for issues that affected minorities. Mfume served as treasurer during his first term in Congress. The CBC gained its strength not only by its number of members but by its representation on committees in Congress.

Junior congressmen do not have much influence. But Mfume was active on the Banking Committee, working to strengthen the hiring of minorities and laws that protect consumers from poor treatment by financial services companies. As a new representative, he worked to fine-tune and support proposals written by other lawmakers. One such proposal called for increased credit for inner-city businesses. This would help African Americans and other minorities arrange for business loans. In many places, white bankers did not like to lend money to minority-owned businesses. Minority-owned businesses were often in poor and dangerous city neighborhoods, and many bankers worried about their investments. The Mfume Amendment to the Competitive Banking and Equality Act called for the federal government to have a plan of action in the development of minority financial institutions. Mfume also sponsored a variety of bills aimed at public housing, job training, and antidrug programs. These bills did not make it through the process to become laws.

During his college years, Mfume had organized protests against the racist government of South Africa. He had educated others about apartheid, South

Africa's system of segregating of the races. Mfume supported the liberation of black South Africans from the laws of the country's white government. South African freedom fighter Nelson Mandela had long been one of Mfume's heroes. In February 1990, Mandela was released from prison after twenty-seven years. A few months later, he visited the United States, where Mfume was honored to be one of the congressmen who accompanied Mandela on part of his tour. Of all the world leaders Mfume met, none meant more to him than Mandela. "I was awestruck and moved nearly to tears at the sight of this man," Mfume later recalled.[2] Over the next year, during Mandela's many visits to the United States as leader of the African National Congress, the two men had many more opportunities to get to know each other.

Congressman Mfume reached out to the public by writing a weekly column for the *Baltimore Afro-American* newspaper. In his column, which ran from 1990 to 1993, Mfume commented on current issues in Baltimore, with topics including bad cops, unfair prison practices, guns on the streets, and kids killing kids.

In Congress, Mfume was a coauthor of the Civil Rights Act of 1991. This important bill was created to revise the Civil Rights Act of 1964 by strengthening and improving federal civil rights laws that ban discrimination in employment. The bill clarified the

Congressman Mfume and the Reverend Jesse Jackson, right, led a protest against discrimination in the workplace.

definition of discrimination and harassment in the workplace. It also provided for monetary settlements for those who won lawsuits against their employers on discrimination issues. An amendment to the bill extended its benefits to U.S. citizens living and working abroad.

One of the purposes of the Civil Rights Act of 1991 was to make it harder for employers to exclude minorities and women from jobs. This meant that everyone was entitled to the same opportunities; it did not reserve jobs for a specific racial or ethnic group. However, opponents of the bill worried that it could force businesses to set quotas—rules dictating how many minorities must be hired. They said qualified whites would lose their jobs so that minority quotas could be met. Using this quota argument, a similar bill had been defeated in 1990. Now, a year later, the congressional debate over the 1991 bill was lively and fierce, and Mfume was in the thick of it. The negotiations went on for months. Finally, the bill was passed, with both sides agreeing that it set rules for equal opportunities, not for quotas.

8

A NEW
POWER POSITION

n Congress, Mfume was known for speaking
out for civil rights, though his primary focus
as a lawmaker had been economic development for the people in his congressional district. In
1992, Mfume was elected chairman of the Congressional Black Caucus (CBC). The organization, founded
in 1970 by thirteen members, had grown into a force
to be reckoned with in Congress. Like Mfume, most of
the members were liberal Democrats. Mfume had been
active in the caucus since his first term in Congress,
when he was treasurer of the organization. In his

Congressman Mfume's primary focus was on helping the people in his district. Here Mfume, right, helped announce the launch of a new program to help Baltimore residents buy homes. Frank Raines of the Federal National Mortgage Association, known as Fannie Mae, was joined by a new homeowner, left. In the back is Baltimore mayor Kurt Schmoke.

second term, he was second vice chairman, and then he moved up to first vice chairman.

After the November 1992 elections, CBC membership had jumped from twenty-six to forty. This gave the organization more political clout than ever before. For decades, African-American lawmakers had been ignored or taken for granted, but this was changing. "I believe our best days are in front of us. Because of the sheer and awesome increase in numbers, we have been given a great opportunity to effectuate real and meaningful change in the House," said Mfume.[1]

The first opportunity for the CBC to flex its new muscle came as the House prepared to vote on whether to give the president a "line-item veto."[2] Without a line-item veto, the president had to accept or reject each congressional bill and all its attachments as one unit. He could not separate the parts. A line-item veto would allow the president to consider each amendment to a bill as a separate piece. This means that after a bill was passed by Congress, the president would be able to pick which parts of the bill he wanted to approve as law—and which parts he wanted to veto, or reject.

Other Democrats and Republicans in Congress were divided on this issue. If the CBC members all decided to vote the same way, their block of forty votes would swing the decision. It was known in Congress that CBC members had concerns about the line-item veto, yet they had not been asked to air their views in the debates. It was assumed that they would simply follow along and pass the bill.

Suddenly it was time to vote on the line-item veto, and the CBC was angry about being ignored. Mfume strode onto the floor of the House of Representatives and announced that the CBC members would not vote on the issue until they were consulted. Later Mfume told the Speaker that the CBC members, as loyal Democrats, insisted on being included in the discussions that shape laws proposed by the Democrats. If not, he said, the CBC would use its voting power against these proposals. The Speaker of the House, knowing these forty votes were crucial, decided to delay the vote on the line-item veto (which, ultimately, was ruled unconstitutional by the Supreme Court). After this showing of CBC power, the House took the caucus much more seriously.

When Clinton reversed his decision about an official appointee, he too learned that the CBC was not a group to overlook. Clinton had announced that he would nominate African-American Lani Guinier, a prominent law professor and NAACP civil rights attorney, to the position of assistant attorney general in the civil rights division. Then questions were raised about her views about affirmative action, the guidelines enforcing equal opportunities for all Americans regardless of race or creed. Guinier's opponents claimed that she supported quotas for hiring minorities. But she had never called for quotas, and the CBC stood strongly by her side. Despite CBC requests, Guinier was not given a hearing in which she could publicly explain her views. Instead, President Clinton formally withdrew Lani Guinier's nomination to the top civil rights job in the nation.

Mfume and the CBC were very angry with President Clinton's decision.[3] They soon used that anger to their advantage when the Clinton administration brought its five-year budget-deficit plan before Congress. The president and the House of Representatives had learned that the forty-member voting bloc of the CBC could make or break the passing of new legislation. The president knew that he would have to listen to the CBC. Unless Clinton met their demands in his budget plan, the CBC members would not support it. The CBC refused to consider Clinton's budget until he promised that he would not cut social assistance programs such as the earned-income tax credit and free immunizations for children who were not covered by health insurance. The CBC also would not accept the president's plan to set limits on the costs of Medicare and Medicaid. When Clinton agreed to CBC terms, the caucus backed his budget, and it passed.

Mfume was maintaining his high profile outside Congress as well. By 1993, he was host of *The Bottom*

As host of *The Bottom Line*, Congressman Mfume invites his television studio audience to speak out.

Line, a locally produced television talk show. Over the years, his weekly show has featured celebrities and a variety of other guests, with discussions targeting schools, health, the role of the police in the community, politics, and other issues.

President Clinton's policies concerning Haitian refugees were another source of conflict with the Congressional Black Caucus. Haiti, a republic in the West Indies, occupies half the island of Hispaniola (the Dominican Republic is the other half). The island is southwest of Cuba. Most Haitians are descendants of black Africans brought there as slaves.

In the early 1990s, Haiti was in turmoil. In 1991, the military overthrew Haiti's president, Jean-Bertrand Aristide, who then fled the country. Supporters of Aristide were beaten, tortured, and killed. Many Haitians tried to escape the country in small boats and rafts, but those who arrived on the shores of the United States were being arrested, imprisoned, and sent back to Haiti.

In his campaign for the presidency, Bill Clinton had promised to end President George Bush's policy of forcing the refugees to return to Haiti. But shortly after the election, President Clinton announced that he, too, would turn Haitian refugees away. Mfume and the CBC were outraged at this violation of human rights. They believed that the only reason Haitians were not being welcomed into the United States was that they were poor and black.

Over the next year, the crisis in Haiti worsened. President Clinton promised to restore Aristide to office; the United States would pressure Haiti's military rulers to step aside. The United Nations imposed economic sanctions—withholding shipments of oil and weapons to Haiti—but this was having no effect on the country's military rulers or on the violence.

On March 18, 1994, the Congressional Black Caucus sent Clinton a letter saying, "The United States' Haiti policy must be scrapped."[4] All forty members of the CBC signed the petition. Five members of the CBC, including Mfume, were arrested when they staged a protest in front of the White House. They wanted everyone to know they disagreed with Clinton's policy toward the nation of Haiti.[5]

Clinton finally agreed that his Haitian policy was a mess. He appointed William Gray, a former member of the CBC, as special envoy to Haiti, and he reversed his decision about immediately sending all Haitian refugees back to their country.[6] Still, it was becoming clear that the Clinton administration would have to make a choice: abandon Aristide or intervene with military force. In the fall of 1994, Clinton finally sent U.S. troops to Haiti to restore order.

In August 1994, the television news magazine *60 Minutes* decided to do a report on Mfume and the mounting influence of the CBC. Mfume was proud of his rise from the streets of Baltimore to the halls of Congress, and he brought the television camera crew to his old neighborhood in West Baltimore. The cameramen followed the well-dressed CBC chairman to the corner of Robert and Division Streets.

Telling the camera crew to stay back, Mfume then walked toward a gang of street thugs, his arms held wide from his body and his coat hanging open.

"Yo, my man, I don't have a gun, and I don't have a badge. It's just me."[7]

The gang surrounded him, their knives flashing, checking him out. Memories flooded Mfume's mind.[8]

Mfume wanted to reach out to young African Americans, as Parren Mitchell had reached out to him years before. He wanted to send the message that if he could rise above his environment, they could, too. As he approached the gang, he explained, "I just want to talk to you brothers. The film crew is just following me because they're doing a bit on me and the 'hood I grew up in."

One of the members called out, "Don't diss me— 'cause I ain't your brother. You think I'm some kind of—fool?"

The last thing Mfume wanted was violence. "No, my man," he replied. "You got the drop on me. I know that—you can't be a fool."[9]

Continuing to use the language of the street, he convinced the leader that he was not there as a threat. He asked the gang members about being in school. When they laughed at him, he said, "So what do you want to do with your life now?"

"I want to have fun," said the leader, as the rest of the gang members nodded and gave one another high fives.[10]

When Mfume suggested that they could "still have fun" if they stayed in school, the mood suddenly changed. The leader pulled out a gun and pointed it toward Mfume's face. "I think I'd rather have fun out here, though," he said. Then, with the gun still cocked and poised, the leader suddenly spoke up, saying he wanted to go into mortuary science. As the young man lowered his gun, the gang burst out laughing, asking him why he wanted to learn about burying dead people. Mfume moved quickly to tell him about a community college program where he could get the training he needed and offered his card.

"Call me at home whenever you're ready and I'll work it out with you," Mfume offered.[11] The gang shot more wisecracks and their leader wheeled around, shaking his fist to reassert his toughness. Mfume slowly walked away, rejoining the *60 Minutes* crew. The young gang leader never did call Mfume.

◆ ◆ ◆ ◆

Under Mfume's leadership, the CBC had become a key force on many important issues. Now, Mfume began planning a leadership summit to work against violence. He wanted many separate organizations to band together on one issue that could benefit the whole African-American community. He invited the NAACP, the Urban League, the Nation of Islam, Jesse Jackson's Rainbow Coalition, black churches, and other organizations to join together to "Stop the Killing." A meeting was held in September 1994 in Washington, D.C., as part of the CBC Legislative Weekend. This annual conference is sponsored by the

Congressional Black Caucus Foundation (CBCF), the fund-raising and educational arm of the CBC.

Mfume spoke about creating alliances between the various African-American groups gathered at the first leadership summit. He wanted them to work together on one common issue—to combat the violence in the streets. But the idea that the CBC was entering into a relationship with the controversial Louis Farrakhan and the Nation of Islam quickly made headlines. Farrakhan has given speeches that insulted Jews, Christians, Asians, women, gays, and other minorities. Not only did Farrakhan receive a great deal of criticism for his speeches, but any group working with him was also criticized. Many black leaders did not like what Farrakhan said and worried that cooperation with the Nation of Islam would hurt their organizations. The NAACP had a long tradition of Jewish support and was especially sensitive to this issue.

Mfume emphasized that working together did not mean groups endorsed one another's beliefs. Each organization still held separate positions on political matters.But the CBC charged that Mfume had acted alone in forming an alliance—that it was not approved by the caucus. Mfume held a news conference to state that the caucus had no official relationship with the Nation of Islam.

At the CBC's Legislative Weekend in 1994, Mfume noted that the number of African Americans at all

NAACP president Ben Chavis talks with reporters at a 1994 press conference. At his side are Congressman Kweisi Mfume, center, and Nation of Islam leader Louis Farrakhan (left, wearing bow tie).

levels of government had grown from fewer than fifteen hundred in 1970 to eight thousand in 1994. Black lawmakers came together in the House of Representatives to discuss bills about crime, health care, and minority businesses. Mfume was concerned about youth, especially young people growing up on the streets, and he was particularly concerned about gun control and education. He said, "We have a major problem with guns on the street and guns in the schools, where drugs are more available than text-books."[12]

Mfume spoke from personal experience when he said that students who drop out of school often drift on the streets in gangs where guns and drugs are a big part of the culture. Without a high school education, young people often have difficulty getting good jobs. A high school diploma, Mfume emphasized, should mean that the student has learned skills to earn a living, and students should not graduate without these skills.[13]

He talked about the need to educate young African Americans, to encourage them to stay in school and to make successes of their lives. He said that African Americans must help themselves, not wait for white Americans to solve black social problems.[14]

Mfume's two-year term as chairman of the Congressional Black Caucus was ending. In January 1995, the Republicans gained the majority in the House of Representatives, cutting funds for legislative caucuses, including the CBC. But the CBC was funded not by the House but by the Congressional Black Caucus Foundation. The Republican majority would not undermine the work of the CBC, Mfume said.[15] Still, without taxpayer funding for the CBC, the caucus had to survive on fewer dollars.[16]

9

BLACK LEADERS
TOGETHER

In 1995, many African Americans were caught up in the plans for a civil rights march and rally to be held in Washington, D.C., on October 16. It was named the Million Man March to remind people of the famous March on Washington led by Martin Luther King, Jr., in 1963.

Although the march was the idea of Louis Farrakhan, leader of the Nation of Islam, many leaders, both black and white, criticized the march because of Farrakhan's involvement. Still, Mfume believed that any effort to unite the black community would have to include the Nation of Islam. He said that blacks would make more progress if "all these groups joined together for a common goal."[1] Despite all the controversy, the march went on as planned, though estimates varied as to the number of participants. Organizers claimed that more than a million African-American men showed up; others put the number at four hundred thousand.

The crowd was peaceful and the mood hopeful. Mfume was there with his sons, other members of the Congressional Black Caucus, and African-American leaders including the Reverend Jesse Jackson. Poet Maya Angelou read a special poem to the huge crowd. Many had waited a long time for such an event. They proclaimed it a chance to help people forget their hostility and work together.[2]

Others were disappointed that the march looked like a celebration. They criticized the leaders for missing an opportunity to talk about solutions to the problems of unemployment, health, education, and housing in their communities. They were disappointed that the leaders did not address the role of churches, religious groups, civic groups, the family, or women.

A month after the march, members of the National Association for the Advancement of Colored People (NAACP) contacted Mfume about the organization's search for a new president. Would Mfume consider taking the helm?

The NAACP is the oldest civil rights group in the

NAACP National Headquarters in Baltimore: In 1995, Mfume was asked to be president of this civil rights organization.

United States. Formed in 1909 by a group of black intellectuals and white liberals, the NAACP has sought to fight racial discrimination through education and legal action. During the 1950s, 1960s, and 1970s, the NAACP won major court battles, helping to integrate schools and public places throughout the United States. Today, the NAACP's main office is on the outskirts of Baltimore, Maryland, and it has half a million members throughout the United States and the world.

NAACP president Benjamin Chavis had been forced to resign in 1994 after charges of sexual and administrative misconduct. The organization was in trouble, with more than $3 million of debt. Its membership, reputation, and effectiveness were in decline.

Mfume thought about the tremendous challenge that the NAACP position would offer. He had been in Congress for ten years and was pleased with his accomplishments there. He had focused congressional attention on a wide range of issues concerning minority business development and civil rights. He had served for two years as chairman of the CBC and then later headed the CBC Task Force to Preserve Affirmative Action.

After a long period of interviewing and negotiating with the NAACP, Mfume accepted the job.[3] On February 15, 1996, Mfume took his position as the chief executive officer and president of the NAACP. President Bill Clinton, Vice President Al Gore, and

Mfume is sworn in as the new president of the NAACP. Looking on are Bill Clinton, president of the United States, and Myrlie Evers-Williams, chairperson of the NAACP board of directors.

Mfume's family stood behind him. Myrlie Evers-Williams, the widow of slain civil rights activist Medgar Evers and chairperson of the board of directors of the NAACP, welcomed Mfume. Under his leadership, Mfume promised, the NAACP would help African Americans and minorities become a strong voting bloc for civil rights.[4] He did not underestimate the job ahead of him. In his acceptance speech, he said

> The NAACP is at a crucial point in its history. In fact, and perhaps, it is at the most critical point. The focus for rebuilding this organization must be on developing new and effective ways of involving young people. It must focus on voter empowerment, which has as its components voter registration, voter education and then voter participation. It must focus in these new days anew on educational excellence and individual responsibility.[5]

10

THE
NAACP

By 1996, when Kweisi Mfume took over as president, the NAACP had an image problem. With few major victories since the 1970s, many people questioned whether the organization was still needed. Even NAACP members themselves often could not agree on the group's priorities. The reports of sexual and administrative misconduct by former NAACP president Benjamin Chavis also tarnished the NAACP's image. Kweisi Mfume faced an extremely difficult job.

Could Mfume turn the troubled NAACP back into a strong organization? As president and chief executive officer (CEO), Mfume would be principal spokesman for the organization. He was in charge of fund-raising, financial planning, and supervision of the staff.

The first challenge was to rescue the NAACP from its staggering $3.2 million debt. Mfume would have to cut staff and raise funds. For this, he used his connections in both the public and private sectors. Hosting his weekly television talk show, *The Bottom Line*, had kept him in the public eye. He was also known from his appearances on cable TV's Black Entertainment Television network, and the newspaper column he used to write for the *Baltimore Afro-American*. Ebony magazine used his picture on its cover, and his face was familiar to millions of people. Mfume's political connections were also well established. "I am one of the few people in the country," he said, "who can call President Clinton and he will answer."[1]

Mfume began working with Myrlie Evers-Williams, chairperson of the board of directors. They agreed to cut staff at national headquarters and reduce budgets at regional offices. Then Mfume appealed to businesses, charitable organizations, and individuals for contributions. By March 1996, only a month after he took over, Mfume had brought in $1 million in donations. By October, just eight months after Mfume became president, the NAACP was out of debt and in the midst of reorganization.

Mfume quickly moved ahead with new projects. He

President Clinton and Myrlie Evers-Williams applaud after the NAACP swearing-in ceremony, as Mfume shares a warm hug with his sons.

planned to develop a $50-million endowment fund for the NAACP. He started antitruancy and school achievement programs in the seventeen hundred NAACP community branches. He also planned to work with other civil rights groups.

At the same time, changes were taking place in the population served by the NAACP. Since the height of the civil rights movement in the late 1950s and 1960s, more African Americans had moved out of poverty and into the middle class. African Americans were also voting in large enough numbers to force state legislatures to set aside more money for urban schools, housing, jobs, and transportation.

"I do not believe the NAACP can or should be all things to all people. . . . What I believe we have to do is find our niche in five or six different areas and do that second to none," Mfume said.[2] Mfume decided the NAACP should concentrate on five areas: civil rights enforcement, voter empowerment, educational excellence, economic empowerment, and youth recruitment.[3]

When Mfume turned his efforts to political and social action issues, his leadership skills received mixed reviews. He was praised for his fiscal management of the NAACP's debt, but he was criticized for not moving quickly and forcefully enough on the civil rights front. For example, when Texaco Oil was accused of discrimination by a group of black workers, Mfume was criticized as being overly cautious. While the Reverend Jesse Jackson called for an immediate boycott of Texaco, Mfume suggested waiting thirty days.[4] Mfume said he wanted to fully understand the situation before he acted, but it was Jackson's quick response that motivated Texaco to give a $176 million settlement to the black workers.[5]

Mfume continued to defend affirmative action. As passed in 1964, the legislation stated:

> No person in the United States shall, on the grounds of race, color or national origin, be excluded from participation in, be denied the benefits of, or be subject to discrimination under any program or activity receiving federal financial assistance.[6]

But affirmative action had been losing favor. Some states, like California and Texas, considered it unconstitutional to force—rather than just encourage—companies to hire minority applicants over other qualified candidates. Instead, lawmakers wanted to see more outreach programs to help workers and students move ahead.

Mfume understood affirmative action in its original form: People should not be discriminated against because of skin color, religious beliefs, or gender; and all people deserve equal opportunities. In 1997, he spoke up for a white teacher who had been laid off by a local school board in New Jersey so an equally qualified black teacher could be hired. "The board [of education] should never have made the decision it made on race," he said.[7]

During the summer of 1997, Mfume addressed educational issues. He opposed government support of private-school students. In this program, the government would distribute vouchers to parents of school-age children, usually in troubled school districts. Parents could use these vouchers toward the cost of tuition in private schools. Mfume said, "Vouchers are a pernicious, steal-from-the poor-and-give-to-the-rich program."[8] He felt that when parents who had money and jobs used vouchers to send their children to private schools, this took money away from educational programs in public schools in poor communities.

NAACP leaders as a whole were divided on this issue. Some, like Mfume, thought that vouchers hurt African Americans, Hispanics, and other poor children because it robbed their communities of funds for local schools. Others believed vouchers would force inner-city schools to improve their programs.

Mfume was also opposed to charter schools—independent public schools run by educators, parents, community leaders, educational businesses, or others. He feared that only the children from financially comfortable homes would apply for admission to charter schools. Very few of these schools were in inner-city communities, and Mfume felt the problem was residential segregation.[9] But younger members of the NAACP disagreed with Mfume. They saw vouchers as an opportunity for children of all races and ethnic groups to attend private schools and charter schools.

In employment, Mfume believed that equal opportunity did not exist, so blacks and minorities needed the affirmative action laws to be enforced.[10] On October 6, 1998, Mfume led a sit-down strike in front of the White House. He protested that the Supreme Court did not hire enough minority court clerks. By law, protesters in front of the White House must continue moving, so when Mfume sat down he was arrested. "Through this civil disobedience, we want to show how passionately we feel about this issue," he said.[11]

Mfume's frontline activism with the NAACP led many people to want him back in politics. For 1999, the city of Baltimore faced a mayoral election without a well-known candidate. Right away, several Baltimore politicians formed a "draft Mfume" campaign.[12] They increased the salary for the position of mayor to entice Mfume to run.

As Mfume began considering his options, his words and actions sent conflicting messages. Despite what he said, he did not appear to be ready to close the door on the possibility of being mayor. By December 1998, Mfume said he was not interested in running, although he did outline his position on the city's needs. By March 1999, he had moved from the suburbs into the city in time to satisfy the residency requirement if, indeed, he decided to run for mayor. Later that month he attended some political rallies, but in April he again said he did not plan to seek election.

At the May 25, 1999, NAACP quarterly meeting, Mfume formally announced his decision not to run for mayor of Baltimore. He was pleased that Baltimore wanted him, but his first priority was the NAACP. He still had a full agenda at the NAACP: "I cannot walk away from that fight at this time."[13]

11

MFUME'S WAY

n 1999, at the ninetieth national convention of the NAACP, Mfume set forth his vision for civil rights. He focused on police brutality and racial profiling, employment opportunities, voter registration, gun control, education, poverty, and affirmative action. During this convention, he was honored by the National Educational Association as an outstanding civil rights leader.

Mfume had already called for President Clinton and Attorney General Janet Reno to put an end to police brutality. He suggested a three-point plan that included withholding money from police departments that had a large number of brutality complaints against them; enforcing the Crime Control Act of 1994, which called for accurate collection of information about a crime; and mandating that police and mayors work together.[1]

Racial profiling—when police officers stop people solely because of their race—was a companion issue. Mfume said police brutality and racial profiling were issues that violated both human rights and civil rights. In March 1999, Mfume and other civil rights activists led a protest march against the police in New York City. Undercover officers had killed a twenty-two-year-old man, firing forty-one shots at the unarmed West African immigrant when they were searching for a rape suspect. Mfume was arrested during the march and led away in handcuffs.

As a result of Mfume's high profile on this issue, he was invited to attend a conference on strengthening relationships between police and the community they served. He praised President Clinton's order for a federal law to force police officers to collect data on the race and gender of people they stop on suspicion or arrest. He called it "a good first step toward eliminating racial profiling by the police."[2]

The NAACP is a watchdog for equal employment opportunities for all citizens. When Mfume considered the low numbers of African Americans, Latinos, and Asians in prime-time television programs, telecommunications, and the hotel industry, he knew it was time for action. By late July 1999, the NAACP issued report cards to the public on the hiring practices of corporations supported by African-American and Latino dollars.[3]

As Mfume and the NAACP brought public awareness to the hiring practices of the entertainment industry, the Fox, CBS, NBC, and ABC networks promised to increase efforts to promote diversity on screen and behind the camera. African Americans make up 13 percent of the United States population. "We think that our presence should be appropriately reflected during prime time and on all levels, in front of the camera as well as behind the scenes," said Mfume.[4] However, in November 2000, the NAACP gave poor grades to the major networks for their diversity efforts. The number of African Americans in television had increased "modestly," but other minorities such as Latinos, Asian Americans, and Native Americans were still "largely excluded."[5]

Gun control had always been an important issue for Mfume, especially during his terms in Congress. In July 1999, the NAACP filed a lawsuit against more than one hundred gun manufacturers. The lawsuit sought to restrict gun sales to dealers with retail stores, to limit sales to one weapon a month per customer, to stop selling handguns to individuals who attend gun shows, and to set up quarterly inspections to see that these recommendations are followed.[6] One unintended result of Mfume's efforts, according to the National Rifle Association—the gun lobby—was that these restrictions would also threaten the civil rights of African Americans who want to buy guns.[7]

As president of the NAACP, Mfume recognized that young people were the strength of his organization. Education leads to jobs, and jobs lead to money and opportunities, helping individuals gain economic independence. But Mfume continued to object to the voucher and charter programs. "Vouchers don't educate, they segregate," Mfume said.[8] Children with affluent and involved parents would use the private-school vouchers and apply for the spaces in charter programs. Poor inner-city children would be left behind. In November 1999, Mfume participated in a panel with other speakers at the Detroit chapter of the NAACP. He agreed with some of them when they said, "The wolves are coming . . . in the shape of vouchers, dressed in sheep's clothing!"[9]

Mfume was also concerned about the low SAT scores of many minority students, which can limit college admissions. To remedy this situation, the NAACP under Mfume's leadership set up SAT-preparation classes. By December 1999, there were classes in eight major cities, including Atlanta, Baltimore, New York, Philadelphia, Miami, and Los Angeles.

At the start of 2000, Mfume's attention was drawn

to a civil rights issue in Charleston, South Carolina, where the Confederate flag flew prominently from the state capitol dome. Sentiments were split between those who believed the flag honored South Carolina's past and those who saw the flag as a symbol of racism and hate. Mfume and other civil rights groups said it demeaned the victims of slavery.

On January 17, 2000, nearly fifty thousand people rallied for the banner's removal. The NAACP said it would maintain its boycott—begun on January 1—of the motion picture and other entertainment industries that filmed or conducted any tourism activities in South Carolina. Mfume's sentiment was clear: "We will continue to march and we will continue to boycott until it flies no more."[10] As a result, the South Carolina Legislature voted to remove the Confederate flag.

In the spring of 2000, Mfume was present for a National Center for Neighborhood Enterprise celebration of seven young men who had not been expected to overcome their backgrounds. These unsung heroes included a former gang leader who gave up violence and turned to community service; a young man born into a poor family of fourteen who founded an academy in Washington, D.C., to help other inner-city youth; and a blind youth who rose above his physical and economic challenges to become a leader in his community.

A prime issue for Mfume and the NAACP continues

to be affirmative action. "We have to talk about racial differences. . . . We have to understand racial stereotypes . . . so that we might be able to change the hearts and minds of people in such a way that in the end, we change the nation," he said.[11] On March 8, 2000, Mfume and other civil rights leaders led fifty thousand demonstrators in Florida in support of that state's affirmative action laws.

In October 2000, Mfume released a study of the banking industry that gave low marks to some banks. The banks were evaluated on several factors: employment, community reinvestment, advertising, vendor development, and charitable giving. Mfume urged African Americans to take their business elsewhere.[12]

Similarly, the NAACP continues to monitor the major hotel chains, urging African-American travelers to avoid staying in those that receive low grades from the NAACP. The hotel industry had promised improvements, but the NAACP report card showed that the hiring of African Americans had not increased.

The NAACP's activities in connection with voting rights reached a peak in November 2000. The organization had been a key component of voting registration drives among African Americans during the fall presidential campaign. The result was a record turnout of voters. "The NAACP spent a tremendous amount of time, money, and energy in a well-organized

NAACP president Kweisi Mfume has been honored as an outstanding civil rights leader.

grassroots campaign to increase the number of African Americans who cast their votes at the polls on Election Day," said Mfume.[13] But in December 2000, the NAACP filed lawsuits on behalf of Florida voters who were discriminated against during the highly disputed presidential election, especially in the heavily African-American districts of West Palm Beach and Miami-Dade.

◆ ◆ ◆ ◆

It was in part to inspire black youth that Mfume in 1996 published his autobiography, *No Free Ride: From the Mean Streets to the Mainstream*. He wrote the book not only to tell his story but also to give hope to other young black men.

Former gang member Mfume now holds honorary doctorate degrees from McHarry Medical College, Morehouse College, Goucher College, Howard University, and Bowie State University. He has received hundreds of awards and citations. Mfume is committed to social service and is a member of Central Maryland's Big Brothers and Big Sisters and other organizations.

Mfume speaks out on important issues and devotes his time and energy to making the NAACP the best it can be. In his first five years as president of the organization, he transformed a $3-million debt into a $3-million surplus in the budget, increased black voter turnout in the South, improved ethnic diversity in the television industry, and led the drive to remove the last Confederate flag flying over a statehouse.

At the start of his second term as NAACP president, Mfume said, "My job isn't finished. I believe this organizaion must do more to bring this nation together, to help define the issues of the day."[14]

Mfume hopes that eventually, after he has completed his work with the NAACP, he can continue in public service as a politician or an educator.[15] Whether or not his political race eventually takes him to the White House, Kweisi Mfume will remain a problem solver. He will continue to work to make the United States of America a better country. He believes that "now is the time. . . to find ways to build bridges one to another, working hardest to bridge those gulfs that are the widest and the most dangerous to cross."[16]

CHRONOLOGY

1948—Frizzell Gray is born on October 24 in Turners Station, near Baltimore.

1953—Enters Fleming Elementary School.

1965—His mother dies of cancer; Frizzell drops out of school.

1972—Completes studies for a general education development diploma (GED); enrolls at the Community College of Baltimore; marries Linda Shields on July 1.

1973—Hosts *Ebony Reflections*, on WEBB radio station; changes his name to Kweisi Mfume.

1974—Enrolls at Morgan State University (Baltimore) as a junior; majors in urban studies.

1976—Graduates magna cum laude from Morgan State.

1979—Elected to Baltimore City Council.

1984—Receives master's degree in political science from Johns Hopkins University.

1986—Elected to Congress as representative from Maryland's Seventh District.

1990—Begins writing weekly column for the *Baltimore Afro-American*.

1991—Is coauthor of the Civil Rights Act of 1991.

1993—Chairs the Congressional Black Caucus (CBC); receives NAACP Leadership Award; begins hosting television show, *The Bottom Line*.

1994—Demonstrates in front of the White House, protesting against President Clinton's Haiti policy.

1996—Cosponsors Americans with Disabilities Act; becomes president and CEO of the NAACP; publishes autobiography, *No Free Ride*.

1997—NAACP issues report cards evaluating hotel and lodging industries' policies affecting minorities.

1998—Leads Million Youth Movement rally in Atlanta.

1999—Works against racism, police brutality, and gun violence; to save affirmative action; and to register voters; plans class-action suit against gun distributors; objects to private-school vouchers; sets up SAT-preparation classes for minority students; NAACP report cards cite failure of television industry to hire and feature minorities; Mfume signs pacts with NBC and ABC and Fox networks to change this.

2000—Heads NAACP boycott of South Carolina tourism industries to protest the flying of the Confederate flag from the state capitol; with other civil rights activists, demonstrates in support of Florida's affirmative action laws; NAACP issues report cards on the banking industry's policies affecting minorities; works to increase minority voters in presidential election; protests discrimination against minority voters in Florida.

Chapter Notes

Chapter 1. Taking Chances, Making Choices

1. Peter Boyer, "The Rise of Kweisi Mfume," *The New Yorker*, August 1, 1994, p. 29.

2. Michael Tuan Bustamante, "Mfume: A Champion," *Call and Post*, December 21, 1995, <http://www.elibrary.com> Infonautics Corporation (April 2, 1999).

3. Kweisi Mfume, "Taking over the NAACP," *Baltimore Afro-American*, December 16, 1995, <http://www.elibrary.com> Infonautics Corporation (April 2, 1999).

4. Author interview with Kweisi Mfume, November 18, 1997.

5. Anthony W. J. McCarthy, "AFRO Was Right: NAACP Chooses Mfume as New President and CEO," *Baltimore Afro-American*, December 16, 1995, <http://www.elibrary.com> Infonautics Corporation (April 3, 1999).

Chapter 2. Growing Up in Turners Station

1. Sherry H. Olson, *Baltimore: the Building of an American City* (Baltimore, Md.: Johns Hopkins University Press, 1980), p. 347.

2. Author interview with Mary Livingston, August 19, 1998.

3. Author interview with Kweisi Mfume, November 18, 1997.

4. Terry Gross interview with Kweisi Mfume, *Fresh Air* (Philadelphia: National Public Radio), July 18, 1997.

5. John Donne, "Devotions Upon Emergent Occasions, Meditation 17," *Norton's Anthology of English Literature* (New York: W. W. Norton & Co., 1962), vol. 1, p. 795.

6. Kweisi Mfume with Ron Stodghill II, *No Free Ride: From the Mean Streets to the Mainstream* (New York: Ballantine Books, 1996), p. 13.

7. Author interview with Kweisi Mfume, November 18, 1997.

8. Author interview with Ronald Turner, August 23, 1998.

9. Author interview with Peggy Patterson, August 19, 1998.

10. Author interview with Mary Livingston, August 19, 1998.

11. Mfume, p. 31.

Chapter 3. West Baltimore

1. Kweisi Mfume with Ron Stodghill II, *No Free Ride: From the Mean Streets to the Mainstream* (New York: Ballantine Books, 1996), p. 57.

2. Ibid., p. 69.

3. Terry Gross interview with Kweisi Mfume, *Fresh Air* (Philadelphia: National Public Radio), July 18, 1997.

4. Author interview with Kweisi Mfume, November 18, 1997.

5. Author interview with Leavonia McKnight, December 3, 1997.

6. Mfume, *No Free Ride*, pp. 56–57.

7. Ibid., pp. 91–93.

8. Ibid., p. 93.

9. Terry Gross interview.

10. Author interview with Kweisi Mfume, November 18, 1997.

11. Mfume, p. 111.

12. Ibid., p. 115.

13. Peter Boyer, "The Rise of Kweisi Mfume," *The New Yorker*, August 1, 1994, pp. 28–29.

14. Author interview with Carl Swann, August 16, 1998.

Chapter 4. Life on the Streets

1. Kweisi Mfume with Ron Stodghill II, *No Free Ride: From the Mean Streets to the Mainstream* (New York: Ballantine Books, 1996), pp. 139–141.

2. Terry Gross interview with Kweisi Mfume, *Fresh Air* (Philadelphia: National Public Radio), July 18, 1997.

3. Ibid.

4. Author interview with Kweisi Mfume, November 18, 1997.

5. Mfume, *No Free Ride*, p. 162.

6. Terry Gross interview.

7. Mfume, *No Free Ride*, pp. 153–154.

8. Terry Gross interview.

9. Peter Boyer, "The Rise of Kweisi Mfume," *The New Yorker*, August 1, 1994, p. 29.

10. Author interview with Kweisi Mfume, November 18, 1997.

Chapter 5. Stepping Forward

1. Author interview with Kweisi Mfume, November 18, 1997.

2. Kweisi Mfume with Ron Stodghill II, *No Free Ride: From the Mean Streets to the Mainstream* (New York: Ballantine Books, 1996), p. 194.

3. Author interview with Kweisi Mfume.

4. Kent Jenkins. "The Baltimore Congressman, with His Eye on the Caucus and His Finger to the Wind," *Washington Post*, December 8, 1992, p. D1.

5. Mfume, *No Free Ride*, pp. 212–213.

Chapter 6. Entering the Public Arena

1. Peter Boyer, "The Rise of Kweisi Mfume," *The New Yorker*, August 1, 1994, p. 30.

2. Author interview with Carl Swann, August 19, 1998.

3. Kweisi Mfume with Ron Stodghill II, *No Free Ride: From the Mean Streets to the Mainstream* (New York: Ballantine Books, 1996), p. 233.

4. Ibid., p. 240.

5. Ibid., p. 245.

6. Author interview with Carl Swann.

7. Mfume, p. 249.

8. Author interview with Carl Swann.

9. Mfume, pp. 260–262.

Chapter 7. Mfume Takes On Congress

1. Kweisi Mfume with Ron Stodghill II, *No Free Ride: From the Mean Streets to the Mainstream* (New York: Ballantine Books, 1996), p. 270.

2. Ibid., p. 312.

Chapter 8. A New Power Position

1. Kent Jenkins, Jr., "Mfume on the Move," *Washington Post*, December 8, 1992, p. D1.

2. Kweisi Mfume with Ron Stodghill II, *No Free Ride: From the Mean Streets to the Mainstream* (New York: Ballantine Books, 1996), p. 322.

3. Ibid., p. 331.

4. Bill Duhart, "U.S. Policy on Haitian Refugees Sparks Protest," *Philadelphia Tribune*, April 5, 1994, <http://www.elibrary.com> Infonautics Corporation (February 15, 1999).

5. James Wright, "Haiti: CBC Members Arrested at White House," *Washington Afro-American*, April 30, 1994.

6. Duhart.

7. Mfume, *No Free Ride*, p. 3.

8. Steve Kroft, "The New Black Power," *60 Minutes*, CBS-TV, September 25, 1994.

9. Ibid.

10. Mfume, *No Free Ride*, p. 5.

11. Ibid., p. 7.

12. Junious R. Stanton, "From the Trenches with Rep. Kweisi Mfume," *Time*, October 31, 1994.

13. Ibid.

14. Vincent Thompson, "Mfume Exits Gracefully as Chairman of CBC," *Philadelphia Tribune*, September 16, 1994, <http://www.elibrary.com> Infonautics Corporation (February 15, 1999).

15. James Wright, "Mfume Denies GOP Will Kill CBC," Washington *Afro-American*, November 26, 1994, <http://www.elibrary.com> Infonautics Corporation (February 15, 1999).

16. Associated Press, "GOP Cuts Steam of Caucus Leader," *Newsday*, December 9, 1994, <http://www.elibrary.com> Infonautics Corporation (February 15, 1999).

Chapter 9. Black Leaders Together

1. Kweisi Mfume with Ron Stodghill II, *No Free Ride: From the Mean Streets to the Mainstream* (New York: Ballantine Books, 1996), p. 345.

2. Gregory Freeman, "Million Man March: 'I Know That This Will Be Part of History,'" *St. Louis Post-Dispatch*, October 15, 1995, p. 6B.

3. Kim Trent, "Leaders Support Mfume," *Michigan Chronicle*, December 26, 1995.

4. William Douglas, "For Blacks, a Shift of Power/Influence Ebbs in Congress, But Focus Flows to Organizing," *Newsday*, December 27, 1995, p. A8.

5. "Remarks by the President and Congressman Kweisi Mfume at the Swearing-in Ceremony for the Honorable Kweisi Mfume as President and CEO of the NAACP," Office of the Secretary, The White House, February 20, 1995.

Chapter 10. The NAACP

1. James Wright, "Hallelujah! Mfume Leaves Congress to Lead NAACP" *Washington Afro-American*, December 16, 1995, <http://www.elibrary.com> Infonautics Corporation (April 15, 1999).

2. Richette Haywood, "Can Kweisi Mfume Turn the NAACP Around?" *Ebony*, January 1997, p. 94.

3. Ibid.

4. Kweisi Mfume, "Mfume's Statement Regarding Texaco," *NAACP Online*, <http://www.naacp.org> (September 19, 1997).

5. Sara Silver, Associated Press, *The News-Times On Line* (Danbury, Conn.) <http://www.newstimes.com/archive97/jan1097/haf.htm> (December 19, 2000).

6. Nat Hentoff, "Affirmative Action Nearing End of Life," *Rocky Mountain News*, November 17, 1997, p. 40A.

7. Scott Simon, "Affirmative Action," *All Things Considered* (Washington, D.C., National Public Radio), November 22, 1997.

8. "Black Leaders Split on Vouchers," *School Reform News*, June 1997.

9. "Like the Times, NAACP's a-Changing." *Philadelphia Daily News*, Philadelphia Online, <http://www.philly.com> (July 17, 1997).

10. "Affirmative Action Must Be Protected," *St. Louis Post Dispatch*, July 14, 1998, <http://www.elibrary.com> Infonautics Corporation (April 15, 1999).

11. Tony Mauro, "Protest Targets Lack of Minority Clerks." *USA Today*, October 2, 1998, p. 13A.

12. Erin Texeira, "Kweisi Mfume's Dance of Indecision," *Baltimore Sun*, May 30, 1999, pp. C1, C4.

13. Michael Janofsky, "NAACP Chief Rules Out Running for Mayor of Baltimore," *The New York Times*, May 25, 1999, p. A19.

Chapter 11. Mfume's Way

1. "NAACP Calls for Presidential Order to Halt Police Brutality Crisis," NAACP press release, February 25, 1999, <http://www.naacp.org/president/release/archives/1999/police_brutality.htm> (December 15, 2000).

2. "Mfume Reacts to President Clinton Order Targeting Racial Profiling," NAACP press release, June 9, 1999, <http://www.naacp.org/president/release/archives/1999/racial-profiling.htm> (December 15, 2000).

3. Xamgba Browne, "NAACP Attacks Mainstream," *New York Amsterdam News*, July 28, 1999, p. 8.

4. "NAACP Blasts TV Networks' Fall Season Whitewash," NAACP press release, July 12, 1999, <http://www.naacp.org/president/releases/naacp_blasts_tv_networks.htm> (December 15, 2000).

5. Greg Braxton, "Minorities Seeing Little TV Diversity," *Los Angeles Times*, November 15, 2000, p. F1.

6. Browne, p. 3.

7. Paul M. Barrett, "NAACP Suit Puts Race on Table in Gun Debate," *Wall Street Journal*, August 13, 1999, p. B1.

8. Evan Thomas and Lynette Clemetson, "A New War Over Vouchers. Poor Parents Want Them, but Civil-Rights Leaders Are Split," *Newsweek*, November 22, 1999.

9. Ibid.

10. Leigh Strope, Associated Press, "Rally Targets S.C. Confederate Flag." World African Network, <http://www.wanonline.com/news/news8758.html> (June 19, 1999).

11. "From Street-Tough, to Congressman to Head of NAACP, Kweisi Mfume Tries to Set Example and Change the Nation," CNN Interactive, October 1, 1998, <http://www.cnn.com/US/9602/mfume/> (June 19, 1999).

12. Laurie Willis, "NAACP Gives Banks 'Report Cards,'" *Baltimore Sun*, October 24, 2000, p. 2C.

13. "NAACP Commends Record Black Voter Turnout in Presidential Race," NAACP press release, November 7, 2000, <http://www.naacp.org/communications/press_releases/record_black_turnout.asp> (December 17, 2000).

14. "Mfume to Stay on as Head of NAACP," Associated Press Online, February 16, 2001, Item No. CX2001047U2931 (March 27, 2001).

15. Author interview with Kweisi Mfume, November 18, 1997.

16. "President Mfume's Remarks to the Goucher College Class of 1997," May 23, 1997, <http://www.naacp.org/president/speeches/archived/goucher.html> (December 17, 2000).

FURTHER READING

Adams, Mike. "Mfume Has Come Far. And He Will Go Farther." *Baltimore Sun*, December 6, 1998, p. C1.

Boyer, Peter J. "The Rise of Kweisi Mfume." *The New Yorker*, August 1, 1994.

Harris, Jacqueline L. *The History and Achievement of the NAACP*. Franklin Watts, 1992.

Hodes, Michael C. "Kweisi Mfume, Marylander of the Year." *Maryland Magazine*, January/February, 1997.

Howe, Rob, Sarah Skolnik, and Don Hamilton. "Bio: The Bookstrap Method Having Salvaged Himself, Kweisi Mfume Strives to Revive the NAACP." *People Weekly*, February 26, 1996, p. 55.

Mfume, Kweisi, with Ron Stodghill II. *No Free Ride, From the Main Streets to the Mainstream*. New York: Ballantine Books, 1996.

INTERNET ADDRESSES

NAACP Online
<http://www.naacp.org/president>

"Kweisi Mfume"
<http://www.africana.com/tt_138.htm>

"Kweisi Mfume, Host of The Bottom Line"
<http://209.196.177.60/tbl/mfume.htm>

"Kweisi Mfume: From Boy in the Hood to Man in the House and Beyond," by James Moody
<http://www.horizonmag.com/2/mfume.htm>

INDEX

Page numbers for photos are in **boldface** type.